Nashida: Visits the Smith Robertson Museum

Moses Meredith Cultural Arts Book Series - Volume 1

A Meredith *Etc* Book

Meredith *Etc*
1052 Maria Court
Jackson, Mississippi 39204-5151
www.meredithetc.com

Copyright © June 5, 2016 Meredith Coleman McGee
Copyright © Second printing Nov. 15, 2017

Loretha Wallace illustrated the 'Nashida' character

All rights reserved. No section of this book may be reproduced or transmitted in any form or by any means, electronic or mechanical including photocopying, recording or by any information storage and retrieval system, without permission in writing from the Publisher.

Published simultaneously in softcover/hardback
Hardback edition 6"x 9" printed by Nook Press
Black and White on Cream paper

Trade paperback 6"x 9" printed by CreateSpace
Black and White on White paper
ISBN-13: 978-0692694800
ISBN-10: 0692694803
54 pages

Meredith Coleman McGee

Nashida

Visits the Smith Robertson Museum

By Meredith Coleman McGee

Photo by Meredith Coleman McGee

Smith Robertson Museum and Cultural Arts Center
Historic Farish Street District
Downtown Jackson
Capital City of Mississippi

Nashida: Visits the Smith Robertson Museum

State historic marker in front of the Smith Robertson Museum

DEDICATION

This book is dedicated to **Smith Robertson**, a former slave from Fayette, Alabama, who migrated to Jackson after the Civil War, became a local barber, the city's first Negro Alderman, and an advocate to educate his race; and to **Pamela Junior, Manager**, Smith Robertson Museum and Cultural Center (1999-2017).

ACKNOWLEDGMENTS

I acknowledge my grandfather Moses Arthur Meredith (1891–1965), known affectionately as "Cap." He and his wives Barbara Nash Meredith (1893-1929) and Roxie Patterson Meredith (1903-86) provided academic, civic, and moral training to their children at home which has influenced the advancement of their offspring.

My grandmother was Roxie. She often told us stories about Black life, Granddaddy Cap and family history; she always had kind words to say about Ms. Barbara.

Meredith Coleman McGee

Meredith Coleman McGee

Nashida

Nashida: Visits the Smith Robertson Museum

```
┌─────────────────────────────────────────┐
│  THIS BOOK IS PRESENTED TO:             │
│                                         │
│                                         │
│                                         │
│  ─────────────────────────────────────  │
│  MOSES MEREDITH CULTURAL ARTS BOOK CLUB, MEMBER │
└─────────────────────────────────────────┘
```

Blog: meredithetc.com

facebook Meredith Etc

Meredith*etc*

Make comments online @
https://meredithetc.com/nashida/

INTRODUCTION

"Mom and dad said I will learn something new every day for the rest of my life," Nashida said.

The above quote from Meredith Coleman McGee's new children's book, NASHIDA: VISITS THE SMITH ROBERTSON MUSEUM points out why books like this one are important; children need to learn something every day and have fun while they are doing it. Congratulations to Meredith C. McGee for creatively weaving the story of Nashida's visit to the Smith Robertson Museum. This book provides information which will inspire the young and the old alike to read, visit and touch history.

There is a huge lack of racial diversity in children's books and media. The Cooperative Children's Book Center at the University of Wisconsin reports that "Of 3,200 books published in 2013 only three percent were authored by black writers and eight percent were about black characters.

The book, NASHIDA: VISITS THE SMITH ROBERTSON MUSEUM fills a void created by the lack of information and guides about black historic people and places. We must nurture the dreams and aspirations of black youth by filling their books and experiences with information which reflect them and their culture.

Teaching children about the historical accomplishments and struggles of African Americans benefits everyone. By connecting children with history, they'll gain a better understanding of themselves and, they will develop cultural pride and compassion for other people.

In NASHIDA: VISITS THE SMITH ROBERTSON MUSEUM Meredith C. McGee creates an environment which honors African American pioneers, landmarks, and events in Black history. This book will engage children with activities that capture their imaginations and fill them with pride.

By Mrs. Dorothy T. Stewart, *Founder*, Women for Progress of Mississippi, Inc.

Nashida: Visits the Smith Robertson Museum

Comment from a descendent of

MOSES ARTHUR (Cap) MEREDITH

I grew up in Detroit, far away from my family in Kosciusko, Mississippi. Even with the great distance between us, my Grandfather Moses (Cap) Meredith, was always discussed; he was described as a very proud man, tall in stature, headstrong and diligent in teaching his children and grandchildren to be proud of their black skin. Their pigment did not make them less than their white counterparts. Cap was an unusual Black man in the south. He purchased his own land and started voting in 1923. He ran a self-sustaining farm and raised his ten children. Cap made sure his children weren't affected by their prejudiced white next-door neighbors. My grandfather's legacy lives on and I'm proud Moses (Cap) Meredith was my grandfather.

Terry Lynn Meredith Street, Daughter of Emmett Meredith, Moses and Barbara's first born.

Emmett was seven years old when his parents moved he, his younger brother Leroy, their baby sister Delma, and the infant girl Thelma on the farm. Owning property expanded the educational opportunities for the Meredith children. Emmett completed the 11th grade at Attala County Training School in 1934 which was as far as the school went that year; the following year he obtained a 12th grade education from CM& I College reaching a remarkable milestone because there were over 177,000 illiterate Negroes in Mississippi.

Note: Meredith Coleman McGee. 2013. *James Meredith: Warrior and the America that created him*. Santa Barbara, California: Praeger Publishing, 18.

Hello beautiful girls, handsome boys, and all readers and learners.

Nashida

My name is Nashida.

I live in Jackson, Mississippi.

I am in the second grade.

My name means "student."

Grandma Nana named me.

Mom and dad said I will learn something new every day for the rest of my life.

After I watched the movie *Selma*, I was surprised about our history; my parents told me they were going to teach me something about my culture and country every Saturday. Mama and daddy showed me a lot of pictures.

Selma supporters protest in front of the White House in 1965
Courtesy of the Library of Congress

Today is Friday; we are going to the Smith Robertson Museum in the morning.

Photo by Carol M. Highsmith. Note: Edmund Pettus Bridge, Selma. Martin Luther King Jr. and others walked over this bridge in 1965. Pres. Barack Obama and others walked across this bridge in 2015.

Photographer Warren K. Leffler. Selma Negroes walked through the streets in 1965 protesting Jim Crow segregation and unjust laws.

Mama read me a bible story about a lady named Ruth. I like a good story. Ruth loved her mother-in-law Naomi. Ruth worked hard. The king was Boaz; he fell in love with Ruth and married her. The story had a happy ending. Mama tucked me into bed. See you in the morning.

Night, Night.

Good morning readers and learners. We had a good breakfast at Grandma Nana and Grandpa's Joe's house. Grandma made cheesy grits, scrambled eggs, sausage, and toast.

Grandma is the boss of the kitchen. When we go to her house we have to wash and dry the dishes. I helped Grandpa put the dishes up.

Now, we are headed to the museum.

Nashida

We're here at the Smith Robertson Museum. It was named after Smith Robertson. He started the first public school for African American children in Jackson in 1894.

African American students attended this school until 1971 when the State of Mississippi obeyed the 1954 *Brown v. Education* U.S. Supreme Court public school desegregation law. The law allowed children of different races to attend school together.

Nashida

The first thing we saw was old wooden desk students used years ago.

We saw a picture of Smith Robertson and W.H. Lanier. Mr. Lanier was the principal of Smith Robertson school from 1912-1929. Lanier High School was named after him.

Pictures and sculptures in the museum are valuable. You can't touch anything.

Photo by <u>Dorothea Lange</u>.
Sharecroppers in Hill House, Mississippi in 1936

A picture of Richard Wright is painted on the wall. He was the smartest student in school in 1925.

When Richard was in the eighth grade the *Jackson Southern Register* a Black newspaper on Farish Street printed his short story. His teachers were very proud of him.

Richard could not check out books in the public library when he was a boy. The library was used by Whites only. But, Richard read a lot of books.

He became a famous writer. He wrote a book called *Black Boy*. His book told readers what it was like to be a black boy 80 years ago. Mama and daddy read it in high school. They attended Calloway.

The two Black boys in the book often stood in the corner of the kitchen watching their mother cook for a White family. They were hungry; but, they couldn't eat. They ate the scraps off the plates when the Whites finished eating. Most days there was only bread left on the plates. Sometimes, a piece of meat was left on a plate. There was plenty of tea. The boys hated being poor.

Richard Wright; photo by Gordon Park.
Students around the world read his books today.

We went upstairs and saw the Africans. One was skinny. They looked sad. The women were half dressed. The men had chains around their necks when they got off the ship.

The people who owned slaves were mean. We put a leash around our dog's neck to walk her. Fluffy eats good. She is not skinny.

Drawing by Scribner, Armstrong, and company. Library of Congress Illus. E178.B92. Slave-coffle passing the White House.

Africans were kidnapped and brought to South and North America in ships against their will. One girl looks like me. I was sad this happened to them.

Back then, women who lived in different communities in African were fashionable. They beaded their hair like we do today.

African women faces reflecting various clans and styles of dress and adornment in the 16th century. Courtesy of the Library of Congress.

I told mama and daddy I didn't want to walk through the ship at the museum. It was dark and the wooden Africans were laying on their sides. Mama and daddy walked through.

Humans were sold on auction blocks.

Courtesy of the Library of Congress

Note: Africans exposed during an auction. The highest bidder paid investors for the right to enslave Africans. The Africans worked for food and shelter and did not earn an hourly wage as people do today. It was hard for them to escape their enslavement (forced labor) because they did not speak English.

Daddy told me slavery was like the story of Moses in the bible. Moses's enslaved relatives build pyramids and palaces for Egyptian kings. Africans built the White House, Mississippi's State Capitol, other mansions, and buildings.

Plantation Mansion, Burkville, Lowndes County, Alabama
Courtesy of the Library of Congress

Moses led the Israelites to freedom. They moved to another city. There were a lot of African American leaders like Harriot Tubman, Frederick Douglass, Martin Luther King, Medgar Evers, and Bob Moses.

President Abraham Lincoln signed the Emancipation Proclamation in 1863 which freed the slaves.

Illustrated by John Serz President Abraham Lincoln holding the Emancipation Proclamation which ended slavery in the USA
- Courtesy of the Library of Congress

Emancipated slaves enrolled in school in New Orleans in 1863

Daddy said after slavery ended, Africans were called freedmen. We were also called Black, Colored, and Negro.

Mama told me Whites in the United States were divided. Some of them wanted us to be full citizens who could check out books from the library and vote. Other Whites wanted us to be second class citizens eating food scraps off their plates.

Some whites donated money and books to create Negro schools.

School for Negros in Henderson County, Kentucky in 1916
Courtesy of the Library of Congress

The Smith Robertson Museum gives visitors a good look at the history of African Americans. Before World War II many Negroes in the south were poor.

Four Negro children dressed in rags posed for a photographer in Natchez, Mississippi in 1927. LC-USZ62-30637

I am enjoying the museum and learning as we go. Daddy told me nobody can ever take knowledge from you. When you read and study, knowledge gets in your brain and it stays there.

Central High School, Little Rock, Arkansas. Photo by Carol M. Highsmith.

Note: Nine Negro students enrolled in Central H.S. in 1957. Little Rock was one of the first cities in the south to follow the *Brown v. Education* law. U.S. Supreme Court justices ordered the schools to desegregate outlawing the "separate but equal" law.

We went to Medgar Evers's room upstairs. He was over the NAACP.

Medgar Wiley Evers, NAACP staff portrait
Courtesy of the Library of Congress

He drove around the state. He investigated violence against Negroes. He fought to end segregation laws.

Tougaloo college students were members of the NAACP Youth Council. Nine of them were arrested by Jackson police in 1961 for trying to use the library on State Street.

"Separate but equal" was the law. It meant different service for African Americans and Whites was fair.

Negroes couldn't use taxis in the 1960s. Photo by Warren K. Leffler
Courtesy of the Library of Congress

I check out books at the Charles Tisdale Library. He was the publisher of the Jackson Advocate. His wife Alice Thomas-Tisdale and daughter DeAnna Tisdale publish his newspaper today.

During segregation, citizens paid a dime to see a movie. Sometimes, African Americans sat in the balcony.

Photo by Marion Post Wolcott. Courtesy of the Library of Congress

Note: Negro man going to the balcony of the Crescent Theatre in Belzoni, Mississippi in 1939. Whites sat on the ground floor. During Reconstruction, Negros sat in the balcony of White churches, and they sat in the balcony of segregated courtrooms.

The Alamo Theatre is one block over on Farish Street. Fifty years ago, it was a movie theatre with one movie screen for African Americans. Movie goers could sit anywhere. Whites attended a different movie show.

The Farish Street Historic District was the first settlement in Jackson for freed Africans after slavery. Lawyers, teachers, preachers, doctors, maids, and barbers lived in the area.

Negro houses in Vicksburg, Mississippi in 1939
Photo courtesy of the Library of Congress.

James Meredith has an exhibit at the museum. In 1962, he became the first dark skinned Negro to attend classes at the University of Mississippi.

Whites started a gun battle with the U.S. government to try to stop his enrollment. President John Kennedy sent the army to the campus. Two people were killed and 100s were injured.

U.S. Marshals in Army trucks patrolling the University of Mississippi's campus September 30, 1962 (the day James Meredith secretly became a student resident on campus). Photo by Jerry Huff.

Daddy bought a book from James Meredith at the library. Mr. Meredith signed his name in daddy's book. A signature is important. I learned how to write in cursive at home. I can sign my signature too.

James Meredith walking on campus escorted by U.S. Marshals October 1, 1962. Photo by Marion S. Trikosko

Photo by Marion S. Trikosko. Soldiers slept in tents in the field across from Baxter Hall where James lived to protect him from violent Whites.

Photo by Marion S. Trikosko. Military vehicle outside of a building at the University of Mississippi, in Oxford, Oct. 4. 1962 (three days after James Meredith integrated the college).

The movie *Selma* opened my mind to our country's history. Mama and daddy's grandparents were farmers. They owned land in Hinds County. My great-grandmothers cooked for their family.

Nashida

Sharecroppers worked on someone else's land. They attended school a few months in the year if they had a school nearby.

My parent's grandparents had an outhouse behind their farm house. Sharecroppers often lived in two to three room houses. Sharecroppers used the bathroom in the woods.

Photo by <u>Dorothea Lange</u>. Rural Hinds County, Mississippi

Sharecroppers worked long hours in the hot fields for low wages.

Sharecroppers picking cotton with storage sacks attached to their shoulders and waists. By sundown, the sacks were full and heavy.

Evicted sharecroppers along Hwy. 60. Photo by Arthur Rothstein Courtesy of the Library of Congress.

Young Whites fought to change laws that discriminated against African Americans. Our race couldn't vote and did not have any representation in our government.

Some protestors use to shout, "Jim Crow must go!"

Photo by Warren K. Leffler. Mississippi Freedom Democratic Party members and supporters protesting discrimination of the Democratic Party toward Negroes outside the Democratic Convention in 1964.

Photo by Warren K. Leffler. Mississippi Freedom Democratic Party members and supporters protesting discrimination of the Democratic Party toward Negroes outside the Democratic Convention in 1964

Nashida

Over 120 years ago Smith Robertson started the first school in Jackson on Bloom Street for African Americans.

Today, the old school site is a museum.

This museum is the first site on the City of Jackson's Civil Rights Driving Tour.

I am glad mama and daddy brought me here.

I learned a lot today.

During slavery it was against the law

to teach African slaves how to read and write.

Reading and learning is one of the most important rights citizens have.

During Jim Crow, public buildings were segregated. African Americans paid taxes but could not check out books from the public library.

Smith Robertson is a pioneer in the field of education in Jackson.

Richard Wright read a lot of books. He was smart; his books told stories about life during his childhood.

Medgar Evers fought in the courts to change laws so African Americans can go to the library, vote, and get good jobs. Mr. Evers helped get Mr. Meredith's case on the NAACP's list.

Mr. Evers was killed in his driveway in 1963 by a White man, who didn't want Mr. Evers changing white culture.

James Meredith opened the college doors for our race in Mississippi. Now, we can study to be anything we want to be.

Fifty years ago, African Americans

could not study to be surgeons, dentists, engineers, or lawyers at Mississippi colleges.

June 5, 1966, James Meredith started a 220 mile *Walk Against Fear* to encourage Negroes to vote and to travel the highways without fear. A White man shot him. Martin Luther King and others finished the walk.

Women fought for equal citizenship rights too. Fannie Lou Hamer, Unita Blackwell, and many others were civil rights workers in the 1960s.

Photo of Fannie Lou Hamer. Courtesy of the Library of Congress

Fannie Lou Hamer, Mississippi Freedom Democratic Party delegate, speaking to the Credential's Committee at the Democratic National Convention, Atlantic City, New Jersey, August 1964 about the harsh reality of Negro life in Mississippi.

Hollis Watkins, Memphis Norman, Anne Moody, Pearlena Lewis, and other Tougaloo college students started the sit-in movement in our state in the 1960s to end Jim Crow at lunch counters.

Back then, Jim Crow rules required African Americans to go to the back of the restaurant on Capital Street to buy a sandwich and a drink. Then, they had to walk down the street and eat and drink.

White customers could sit down at the counter, rest, and eat.

The United States congress voted to give freedmen voting rights in 1870. A mulatto freedman named John Roy Lynch from Natchez was elected to state government in 1871.

The shackle broken - by the genius of freedom by E. Sachse & Co

The 1890 Mississippi Constitution removed the voting rights of Negro men.

An African American named Robert Clark from Holmes County was elected to state government in 1968.

Unita Blackwell became the first African American women elected as a mayor of a Mississippi city in 1976.

Alyce Clarke become the first African American woman elected to the state legislature in 1985.

Next week, we are going to the Mississippi State Capitol a few blocks away on High Street.

The State Capital is the second site on the city's Civil Rights driving tour.

One Saturday, we are going to meet an artist.

You got to come to the museum!

Nashida

Learning history is fun.

THE END

Advance Praise for *Nashida: Visits the Smith Robertson Museum*

Meredith Coleman McGee has penned a book that needs to be required reading for all Mississippi's 3rd graders, especially those in the Jackson Public Schools. The print is large, the images historically support the script, and the length is age appropriate. *Nashida* discussed the African American past in an interesting manner, one which will allow young readers to ask questions. Well done, Meredith.

J. Moffett Walker, *Author, Retired Counselor/Educator, President & Cofounder*, Clinton Ink-Slingers

I truly enjoyed reading *Nashida: Visits the Smith Robertson Museum*," an educational children's book, by my cousin Meredith Coleman McGee. Students can learn many historical events that occurred mainly in the south between The Emancipation Proclamation and the Civil Rights era. The Smith Robertson Museum is an important resource for families; this book is perfect for school libraries and classrooms.

Theatrice Meredith-Mott, *Librarian/Teacher*

Meredith Coleman McGee, a seminal thinker, showed that parents are teachers, and the profoundly important role they play in passing on knowledge to free born children about courageous African Americans. Equipped with the knowledge that African American role models were honest, courageous, pioneers, enhances children's ability to be critical thinkers which is so important for a free people.

Dorothy Benford, *Historian*

I hope the **Smith Robertson Museum** is on the list of every family's Black History Tour. *Nashida: Visits the Smith Robertson Museum* is a beautiful introduction to the museum with a very personal touch. After reading the book, I am already planning a trip to the Historic Farish Street area of Jackson, Mississippi to visit this museum that salutes so many giants of history within its walls. Meredith Coleman McGee has once again proven that she is a skilled leader in using the written word for the common good.

Alice Paris, *Community Activist*

Nashida: Visits the Smith Robertson Museum is one of the best historical and academic children books I have ever read. It is full with local knowledge of African Americans who made significant contributions to society. It provides evidence of the struggles of Black Mississippians and depicts what life was like during slavery and segregation. Illustrations and pictures guide readers understand of the written words. The book gives children the sense that they can overcome anything, no matter the situation, with knowledge and hard work. This book will make Black children feel relevant and proud of their heritage. Is a must read for children of all ages.

Brenda Hyde, *Community Educator*

Nashida: Visits the Smith Robertson Museum will inspire young readers to seek knowledge in their own backyards. What an excellent way to present African American history through the eyes of this second grader. Readers are taken through Nashida's thought process as she internalizes everything she sees at the museum. This was an easy and enjoyable read for young and old readers. Our 6th grader read it to our kindergartner and they both enjoyed it!

Jackson City Councilman Tyrone Hendrix and **Ercilla Dometz-Hendrix**, *Founders*, South Jackson Proud Community Development Corporation

Other books by Meredith Coleman McGee:

Nashida: Visits the Mississippi State Capitol
Odyssey (Poetry, Articles, Leadership Study)
James Meredith Warrior and the America that created him (Biography)
Married to Sin (Memoir about Darlene Collier)
Casada al Pecado Spanish translation of *Married to Sin*

Meredith
A small press
Meredithetc.com

Nashida
Visits the Mississippi State Capitol

By Meredith Coleman McGee
Moses Meredith Cultural Arts Series Vol. 2

Eight-year-old Nashida shares stories about the legacy of four former Mississippi governors including Andrew Longino (1900-1904); James Kimble Vardaman (1904-1908); Edmond Favor Noel (1908-1912); and Earl Leroy Brewer (1912-1916) with young readers. Nashida also describes the responsibilities of lawmakers in the context of her tour of the Mississippi State Capitol. Readers will learn how a bill becomes law and historical information about the state of Mississippi. Readers and learners will walk away with an understanding of how state laws impact theirs lives and the people who live in their communities.

August 18, 2017, 90 pages
Trade paperback, e-book, hardback
ISBN-13: 978-0692694800
Softcover $9.99 most retailers
Hardback $14.99 (Ingram/Meredithetc.com)
ISBN-13: 978-0-9993226-0-4
E-book $3.99 Kindle
Genre: Children's chapter book
Subject: history/culture/government

Product Page ###

Make comments online @
https://meredithetc.com/nashida-2/

Note: Nashida is a fictional character who shares history, culture, and lessons about the arts and service with young readers.

Meredith & Children Books:

My Brother J-Boy by Hazel Janell Meredith
Illustrated by Chuck Justo

Saving the Manatees by JaNiya Williams
Illustrated by Calla Ridgeway

My First Book Series:
Community Library Initiative

My 1 to 5 Activity Book
My A to G Activity Book
My H to P Activity Book

Join the conversation @ https://meredithetc.com/nashida/

Nashida

www.ingramcontent.com/pod-product-compliance
Lightning Source LLC
Chambersburg PA
CBHW061259040426
42444CB00010B/2431